**BRITISH MUSEUM.**

The

# Babylonian Story of the Deluge

and the

# Epic of Gilgamish

*With an Account of the Royal Libraries of Nineveh*

WITH EIGHTEEN ILLUSTRATIONS

PRINTED BY ORDER OF THE TRUSTEES.

1920.

PRICE ONE SHILLING.

[All Rights Reserved.]

# THE BABYLONIAN STORY OF THE DELUGE AS TOLD BY ASSYRIAN TABLETS FROM NINEVEH.

### THE DISCOVERY OF THE TABLETS AT NINEVEH BY LAYARD, RASSAM AND SMITH.

IN 1845–47 and again in 1849–51 Mr. (later Sir) A. H. Layard carried out a series of excavations among the ruins of the ancient city of Nineveh, "that great city, wherein are more "than sixteen thousand persons that cannot discern between "their right hand and their left; and *also* much cattle" (Jonah iv, 11). Its ruins lie on the left or east bank of the Tigris, exactly opposite the town of Al-Mawṣil, or Môṣul, which was founded by the Sassanians and marks the site of Western Nineveh. At first Layard thought that these ruins were not those of Nineveh, which he placed at Nimrûd, about 20 miles downstream, but of one of the other cities that were builded by Asshur (*see* Gen. x, 11, 12). Thanks, however, to Christian, Roman and Muḥammadan tradition, there is no room for doubt about it, and the site of Nineveh has always been known. The fortress which the Arabs built there in the seventh century was known as "Ḳal'at Nînawî," *i.e.*, "Nineveh Castle," for many centuries, and all the Arab geographers agree in saying that the mounds opposite Môṣul contain the ruins of the palaces and walls of Nineveh. And few of them fail to mention that close by them is "Tall Nabi Yûnis," *i.e.*, the Hill from which the Prophet Jonah preached repentance to the inhabitants of Nineveh, that "exceeding "great city of three days' journey" (Jonah iii, 3). Local tradition also declares that the prophet was buried in the Hill, and his supposed tomb is shown there to this day.

### THE WALLS AND PALACES OF NINEVEH.

The situation of the ruins of the palaces of Nineveh is well shown by the accompanying reproduction of the plan of the city made by Commander Felix Jones, I.N. The remains of the older palaces built by Sargon II (B.C. 721–705), Sennacherib (B.C. 705–681), and Esarhaddon (B.C. 681–668) lie under the hill called Nabi Yûnis, and those of the palaces and other buildings of Ashur-bani-pal (B.C. 681–626) under the mound which is known locally as " Tall al-'Armûshîyah," *i.e.*, " The " Hill of 'Armûsh," and " Ḳuyûnjiḳ." The latter name is said to be derived from two Turkish words meaning " many sheep," in allusion to the large flocks of sheep that find their pasture on and about the mound in the early spring. These two great mounds lie close to the remains of the great west wall of Nineveh, which in the time of the last Assyrian Empire was washed by the waters of the river Tigris. At some unknown period the course of the river changed, and it is now more than a mile distant from the city wall. The river Khausur, or Khoser, divides the area of Nineveh into two parts, and passing close to the southern end of Ḳuyûnjiḳ empties itself into the Tigris. The ruins of the walls of Nineveh show that the east wall was 16,000 feet long, the north wall 7,000 feet long, the west wall 13,600 feet, and the south wall 3,000 feet; its circuit was about 13,200 yards or $7\frac{1}{2}$ miles.

### Discovery of the Library of the Temple of Nebo at Nineveh.

In the spring of 1852 Layard, assisted by H. Rassam, continued the excavation of the " South West Palace " at Ḳuyûnjiḳ. In one part of the building he found two small chambers, opening into each other, which he called the " chamber of records," or " the house of the rolls." He gave them this name because " to the height of a foot or more from the floor they were entirely filled " with inscribed baked clay tablets and fragments of tablets. Some tablets were complete, but by far the larger number of them had been broken up into many fragments, probably by the falling in of the roof and upper parts of the walls of the buildings when the city was pillaged and set on fire by the Medes and Babylonians. The tablets that were kept in these chambers numbered many thousands. Besides those that were found in them by Layard, large numbers have been dug out all along

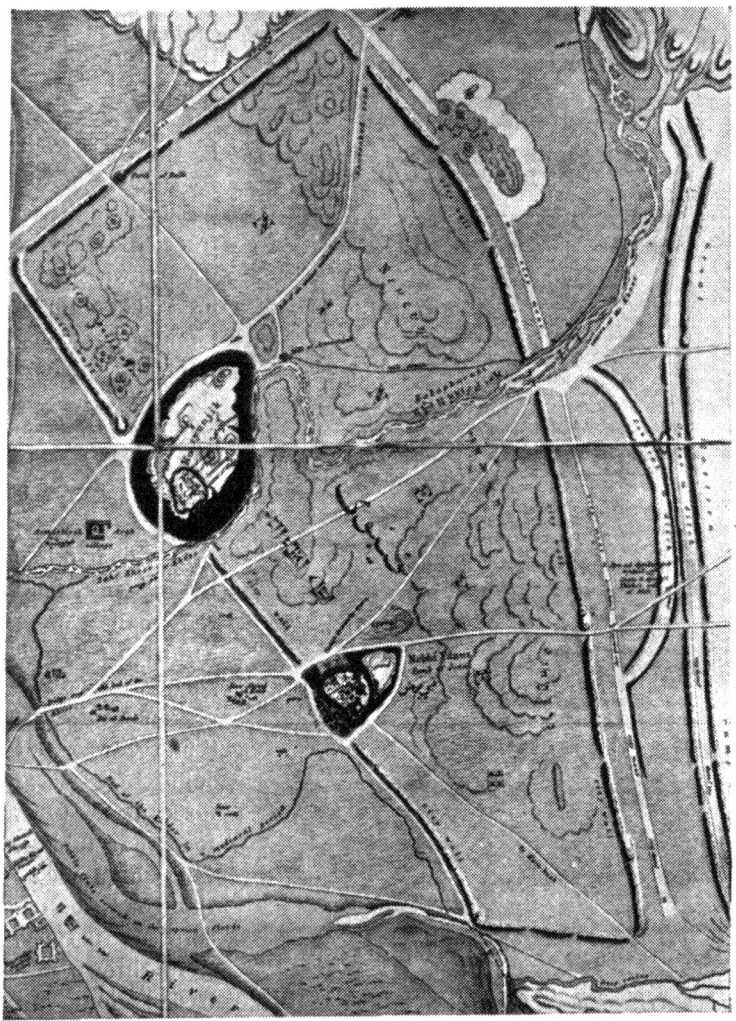

Plan of the ruins of the walls, temples and palaces of Nineveh, showing the course of the River Khausur, and the great protective ditches outside the eastern wall. The southern mound (Nabi Yûnis) contains the ruins of palaces, etc., built by Sargon II, Sennacherib and Esarhaddon, and the northern mound (Kuyûnjik) the Palaces and Library of Ashur-bani-pal, the Library of Nebo, etc. *From the drawing made by the late Commander Felix Jones, I.N.*

## 4  THE BABYLONIAN STORY OF THE DELUGE.

the corridor which passed the chambers and led to the river, and a considerable number were kicked on to the river front by the feet of the terrified fugitives from the palace when it was set on fire. The tablets found by Layard were of different sizes; the largest were rectangular, flat on one side and convex on the other, and measured about 9 ins. by 6½ ins., and the smallest were about an inch square. The importance of this "find" was not sufficiently recognized at the time, for the tablets, which were thought to be decorated pottery, were thrown into baskets and sent down the river loose on rafts to Baṣrah, whence they were despatched to England on a British

Baked clay cylinder of Sennacherib, King of Assyria, from B.C. 705 to 681, inscribed with an account of eight campaigns of the king, including the capture and sack of Babylon, the invasion of Palestine, and the siege of Jerusalem; it is dated in the eponymy of Bel-imurani, i.e., B.C. 691. B.M. No. 91,032. This cylinder was found among the ruins of a palace of Sennacherib under the mound of Nabi Yūnis, and was bought by Colonel J. Taylor, Consul-General of Baghdâd in 1830, from whose representatives it was bought by the Trustees of the British Museum in 1855.

# HISTORICAL CYLINDERS FROM NABI YÛNIS.

Baked clay six-sided cylinder, inscribed with the Annals of Esarhaddon, King of Assyria, from B.C. 681–668. B.M. No. 91,028. This cylinder was found in the ruins of the palace of Esarhaddon, under the mound of Nabi Yûnis, and had been "used as a candlestick by a respectable Turcoman family living in the village on the mound near the tomb of the prophet [Jonah]." The grease marks from the candles are still visible on it. It was acquired by Sir Henry Layard and presented by him to the British Museum in 1848.

man o' war. During their transport from Nineveh to England they suffered more damage from want of packing than they had suffered from the wrath of the Medes. Among the complete tablets that were found in the two chambers several had colophons inscribed or scratched upon them, and when these were deciphered by Rawlinson, Hincks and Oppert a few years later, it became evident that they had formed part of the library of the TEMPLE OF NEBO AT NINEVEH.

### NEBO AND HIS LIBRARY AT NINEVEH.

Nothing is known of the early history of the Library[1] of the Temple of Nebo at Nineveh. There is little doubt that it was in existence in the reign of Sargon II, and it was probably founded at the instance of the priests of Nebo who were settled at Nimrûd (the Calah of Gen. x, 11), about 20 miles downstream of Nineveh. Authorities differ in their estimate of the attributes that were assigned to Nebo (𒀭𒀝 Nabu) in Pre-Babylonian times, and cannot decide whether he was a water-god, or a fire-god, or a corn-god, but he was undoubtedly associated with Marduk, either as his son or as a fellow-god. It is certain that as early as B.C. 2000 he was regarded as one of the "Great Gods" of Babylonia, and about 1,200 years later his cult was general in Assyria. He had a temple at Nimrûd in the ninth century B.C., and King Adad-Nirari (B.C. 811–783) set up six statues in it to the honour of the god; two of these statues are now in the British Museum. Under the last Assyrian Empire he was believed to possess the wisdom of all the gods, and to be the "All-wise" and "All-knowing." He was the inventor of all the arts and sciences, and the source of inspiration in wise and learned men, and he was the divine scribe and past master of all the mysteries connected with literature and the art of writing (𒁾 𒊬 𒊑, duppu sharrute). Ashur-bani-pal addresses him as "Nebo, the bene-"ficent son, the director of the hosts of heaven and of earth, "holder of the tablet of knowledge, bearer of the writing-reed "of destiny, lengthener of days, vivifier of the dead, stablisher "of light for the men who are troubled" (see tablet R.M. 132)

---

[1] A group of Sumerian words for "library" are 𒄑𒁺𒀀 (girginakku), and these seem to mean "collection of writings."

In the reign of Sargon II the temple library of Nebo was probably housed in some building at or near Nabi Yûnis, or, as George Smith thought, near Ḳuyûnjiḳ, or at Ḳuyûnjiḳ itself. As Layard found the remains of Nebo's Library in the South West Palace, it is probable that Ashur-bani-pal built a new temple to Nebo there and had the library transferred to it. Nebo's temple at Nineveh bore the same name as his very ancient temple at Borsippa (the modern Birs-i-Nimrûd), viz., "E-Zida."

Discovery of the Palace Library of Ashur-bani-pal.

In the spring of 1852 Layard was obliged to close his excavations for want of funds, and he returned to England with Rassam, leaving all the northern half of the great mound of Ḳuyûnjiḳ unexcavated. He resigned his position as Director of Excavations to the Trustees of the British Museum, and Colonel (later Sir) H. C. Rawlinson, Consul-General of Baghdâd, undertook to direct any further excavations that might be possible to carry out later on. During the summer the Trustees received a further grant from Parliament for excavations in Assyria, and they dispatched Rassam to finish the exploration of Ḳuyûnjiḳ, knowing that the lease of the mound of Ḳuyûnjiḳ for excavation purposes which he had obtained from its owner had several years to run. When Rassam arrived at Môṣul in 1853, and was collecting his men for work, he discovered that Rawlinson, who knew nothing about the lease of the mound which Rassam held, had given the French Consul, M. Place, permission to excavate the northern half of the mound, *i.e.*, that part of it which he was most anxious to excavate for the British Museum. He protested, but in vain, and, finding that M. Place intended to hold Rawlinson to his word, devoted himself to clearing out part of the South West Palace which Layard had attacked in 1852. Meanwhile M. Place was busily occupied with the French excavations at Khorsabad, a mound which contained the ruins of the great palace of Sargon II, and had no time to open up excavations at Ḳuyûnjik. In this way a year passed, and as M. Place made no sign that he was going to excavate at Ḳuyûnjiḳ, and Rassam's time for returning to England was drawing near, the owner of the

SPECIMENS OF TABLETS FROM NINEVEH.

1. Astrological report concerning divinations of the Moon.
2. Astrological report concerning the Moon and Mercury.
3. Prayers of Ashur-bani-pal to Nebo.

SPECIMENS OF TABLETS FROM NINEVEH.

1. Part of a mythological legend concerning early Babylonian rulers.
2. Assyrian letter.
3 and 4. Letter and envelope from Ashur-ritsûa to an official.

SPECIMENS OF TABLETS FROM NINEVEH.

1. Catalogue of Omen tablets, giving the first line of each.
2. Contract tablet, written B.C. 675.
3. Contract tablet, with the impression of a seal; written B.C. 693.
4. Contract tablet, written B.C. 686.

Explanatory List of Words with glosses.

## 12 SPECIMENS OF TABLETS FROM NINEVEH.

1. Label, inscribed with the title of a series of astrological forecasts.
2. Label, inscribed with the title of a series of omens.
3. Part of a text containing grammatical paradigms.

mound, who was anxious to get the excavations finished so that he might again graze his flocks on the mound, urged Rassam to get to work in spite of Rawlinson's agreement with M. Place. He and Rassam made arrangements to excavate the northern part of the mound clandestinely and by night, and on 20th December, 1853, the work began. On the first night nothing of importance was found ; on the second night the men uncovered a portion of a large bas-relief ; and on the third night a huge mass of earth collapsed revealing a very fine bas-relief, sculptured with a scene representing Ashur-bani-pal standing in his chariot. The news of the discovery was quickly carried to all parts of the neighbourhood, and as it was impossible to keep the diggings secret any longer, the work was continued openly and by day. The last-mentioned bas-relief was one of the series that lined the chamber, which was 50 feet long and 15 feet wide, and illustrated a royal lion hunt.[1] This series, that is to say, all of it that the fire which destroyed the palace had spared, is now in the British Museum (*see* the Gallery of the Assyrian Saloon).

Whilst the workmen were clearing out the Chamber of the Lion Hunt they came across several heaps of inscribed baked clay tablets of " all shapes and sizes," which resembled in general appearance the tablets that Layard had found in the South West Palace the year before. There were no remains with them, or near them, that suggested they had been arranged systematically and stored in the Chamber of the Lion Hunt, and it seems as if they had been brought there from another place and thrown down hastily, for nearly all of them were broken into small pieces. As some of them bore traces of having been exposed to great heat they must have been in that chamber during the burning of the palace. When the tablets were brought to England and were examined by Rawlinson, it was found from the information supplied by the colophons that they formed a part of the great PRIVATE LIBRARY OF

---

[1] These bas-reliefs show that lions were kept in cages in Nineveh and let out to be killed by the King with his own hand. There seems to be an allusion to the caged lions by Nahum (ii. 11) who says, " Where s the dwelling of the lions, and the feeding place of the young lions, where the lion, *even* the old lion, walked, *and* the lion's whelp, and none made *them* afraid ? "

## 14   THE BABYLONIAN STORY OF THE DELUGE.

ASHUR-BANI-PAL, which that king kept in his palace. The tablets found by Layard in 1852 and by Rassam in 1853 form the unique and magnificent collection of cuneiform tablets in the British Museum, which is now commonly known as the "Kuyûnjik Collection." The approximate number of the inscribed baked clay tablets and fragments that have come from Kuyûnjik and are now in the British Museum is 25,073. It is impossible to over-estimate their importance and value from religious, historical and literary points of view; besides this, they have supplied the material for the decipherment of cuneiform inscriptions in the Assyrian, Babylonian and Sumerian languages, and form the foundation of the science of Assyriology which has been built up with such conspicuous success during the last 70 years.

### ASHUR-BANI-PAL, BOOK-COLLECTOR AND PATRON OF LEARNING.

Ashur-bani-pal (the Asnapper of Ezra iv, 10) succeeded his father Esarhaddon B.C. 668, and at a comparatively early period of his reign he seems to have devoted himself to the study of the history of his country, and to the making of a great Private Library. The tablets that have come down to us prove not only that he was as great a benefactor of the Library of the Temple of Nebo as any of his predecessors, but that he was himself an educated man, a lover of learning, and a patron of the literary folk of his day. In the introduction to his Annals as found inscribed on his great ten-sided cylinder in the British Museum he tells us how he took up his abode in the chambers of the palace from which Sennacherib and Esarhaddon had ruled the Assyrian Empire, and in describing his own education he says:

"I, Ashur-bani-pal, within it (*i.e.*, the palace) understood "the wisdom of Nebo, all the art of writing of every crafts-"man, of every kind, I made myself master of them all (*i.e.*, "of the various kinds of writing)."[1]

[1] 𒀭𒀸𒋩𒁀𒉌𒀊𒇴 ... (Brit. Mus., No. 91,026, Col. 1, ll. 31–33).

Baked clay ten-sided cylinder inscribed with a description of the most important events of the reign of Ashur-bani-pal, king of Assyria, B.C. 668-626, and an account of the building operations which he carried on in Nineveh. B.M. No. 91,026. This cylinder was discovered in a chamber in one of the main walls of the palace of Ashur-bani-pal at Nineveh by Mr. Hormuzd Rassam in 1878.

## 16    THE BABYLONIAN STORY OF THE DELUGE.

These words suggest that Ashur-bani-pal could not only read cuneiform texts, but could write like a skilled scribe, and that he also understood all the details connected with the

Scene on bas-relief from a chamber in the palace of Ashur-bani-pal at Nineveh, in which the king is represented standing before a table of offerings and a divine symbol and pouring out a libation over a group of dead lions.   Assyrian Saloon, No. 118.

# SUMERIAN LITERATURE. 17

craft of making and baking tablets. Having determined to form a Library in his palace he set to work in a systematic manner to collect literary works. He sent scribes to ancient seats of learning, *e.g.*, Ashur, Babylon, Cuthah, Nippur, Akkad, Erech, to make copies of the ancient works that were preserved there, and when the copies came to Nineveh he either made transcripts of them himself, or caused his scribes to do so for the Palace Library. In any case he collated the texts himself and revised them before placing them in his Library. The appearance of the tablets from his Library suggests that he established a factory in which the clay was cleaned and kneaded and made into homogeneous, well-shaped tablets, and a kiln in which they were baked, after they had been inscribed. The uniformity of the script upon them is very remarkable, and texts with mistakes in them are rarely found. How the tablets were arranged in the Library is not known, but certainly groups were catalogued, and some tablets were labelled.[1] Groups of tablets were arranged in numbered series, with " catch lines," the first tablet of the series giving the first line of the second tablet, the second tablet giving the first line of the third tablet, and so on.

Ashur-bani-pal was greatly interested in the literature of the Sumerians, *i.e.*, the non-Semitic people who occupied Lower Babylonia about B.C. 3500 and later. He and his scribes made bilingual lists of signs and words and objects of all classes and kinds, all of which are of priceless value to the modern student of the Sumerian and Assyrian languages. Annexed is an extract from a List of

Extract from a List of Signs with Sumerian and Assyrian values. From Rawlinson, *Cuneiform Inscriptions of Western Asia*, Vol. II, Plate I, ll. 155-168.

---

[1] K. 1352 is a good specimen of a catalogue (see p. 10); K. 1400 and K. 1539 are labels (see p. 12).

## 18  THE BABYLONIAN STORY OF THE DELUGE.

Signs with Sumerian and Assyrian values. The signs of which the meanings are given are in the middle column; the Sumerian values are given in the column to the left, and their meanings in Assyrian in the column to the right. To many of his copies of Sumerian hymns, incantations, magical formulas, etc., Ashur-bani-pal caused interlinear translations to be added in Assyrian, and of such bilingual documents the following extract from a text relating to the Seven Evil Spirits will serve as a specimen. The 1st, 3rd, 5th, etc., lines are written in Sumerian, and the 2nd, 4th, 6th, etc., lines in Assyrian.

Extract from a tablet containing a text relating to the Seven Evil Spirits, written in the Sumerian language, with an interlinear translation in Assyrian. From Rawlinson, *Cuneiform Inscriptions of Western Asia*, Vol. IV, Plate XV, Obverse, ll. 33-46 (K. 111—K. 2754).

The tablets that belonged to Ashur-bani-pal's private Library and those of the Temple of Nebo can be distinguished by the colophons, when these exist. Two forms of colophon for each class of the two great collections of tablets are known, one short and one long. The short colophon on the tablets of the King's Library reads :—" Palace of Ashur-bani-pal, "king of hosts, king of the country of Assyria", and that on the tablets of the Library of Nebo reads :—" [Country of ?] Ashur-bani-pal, king "of hosts, king of the country of Assyria". See on the Tablet of Astrological Omens,

p. 22. The longer colophons are of considerable interest and renderings of two typical examples are here appended:—

1. COLOPHON OF THE TABLETS OF THE PALACE LIBRARY.
(K. 4870.)

Colophon of a tablet from the Palace Library of Ashur-bani-pal containing incantations in the Sumerian language, with interlinear translations in Assyrian. For an English rendering see following page. From Rawlinson, *Cuneiform Inscriptions of Western Asia*, Vol. IV, Plate VI, col. 6 (K. 4870).

1. Palace of Ashur-bani-pal, king of hosts, king of the country of Assyria,
2. who trusteth in the god Ashur and the goddess Bêlit,
3. on whom the god Nebo (Nabû) and the goddess Tasmetu
4. have bestowed all-hearing ears
5. and his possession of eyes that are clearsighted,
6. and the finest results of the art of writing
7. which, among the kings who have gone before,
8. no one ever acquired that craft.
9. The wisdom of Nebo [as expressed in] writing, of every kind,
10. on tablets I wrote, collated and revised,
11. [and] for examination and reading
12. in my palace I placed—[I]
13. the prince who knoweth the light of the king of the gods, Ashur.
14. Whosoever shall carry [them] off, or his name side by side with mine
15. shall write may Ashur and Bêlit wrathfully
16. sweep away, and his name and his seed destroy in the land.

2. COLOPHON OF THE TABLETS OF THE LIBRARY OF NEBO.
(RM. 132.)

1. To Nebo, beneficent son, director of the hosts of heaven and of earth,
2. holder of the tablet of knowledge, he who hath grasped the writing reed of destinies,
3. lengthener of days, vivifier of the dead, stablisher of light for the men who are perplexed,
4. [from] the great lord, the noble Ashur-bani-pal, the lord, the approved of the gods Ashur, Bêl and Nebo,
5. the shepherd, the maintainer of the holy places of the great gods, stablisher of their revenues,
6. son of Esarhaddon, king of hosts, king of Assyria,
7. grandson of Sennacherib, king of hosts, king of Assyria,
8. for the life of his souls, length of his days, [and] well-being of his posterity,
9. to make permanent the foundation of his royal throne, to hear his supplications,

10. to receive his petitions, to deliver into his hands the rebellious.
11. The wisdom of Ea, the precious priesthood, the leadership,
12. what is composed for the contentment of the heart of the great gods,
13. I wrote upon tablets, I collated, I revised
14. literally according to all the tablets of the lands of Ashur and Akkad,
15. and I placed in the Library of E-Zida, the temple of Nebo my lord, which is in Nineveh.
16. O Nebo, lord of the hosts of heaven and of earth, look upon that Library joyfully for years (*i.e.*, for ever).
17. Of Ashur-bani-pal, the chief, the worshipper of thy divinity, daily the reward of the offering—
18. his life decree, so that he may exalt thy great godhead.

The tablets from both Libraries when unbroken vary in size from 15 inches by 8⅝ inches to 1 inch by ⅞-inch, and they are usually about 1 inch thick. In shape they are rectangular, the obverse being flat and the reverse slightly convex. Contract tablets, letter tablets and "case" tablets are very much smaller, and resemble small pillows in shape. The principal subjects dealt with in the tablets are history, annalistic or summaries, letters, despatches, reports, oracles, prayers, contracts, deeds of sale of land, produce, cattle, slaves, agreements, dowries, bonds for interest (with impressions of seals, and fingernails, or nail marks), chronography, chronology, Canons of Eponyms, astrology (forecasts, omens, divinations, charms, spells, incantations), mythology, legends, grammar, law, geography, etc.[1]

## GEORGE SMITH'S DISCOVERY OF THE EPIC OF GILGAMISH AND THE STORY OF THE DELUGE.

The mass of tablets which had been discovered by Layard and Rassam at Nineveh came to the British Museum in

---

[1] For a full description of the general contents of the two great Libraries of Nineveh, see Bezold, *Catalogue of the Cuneiform Tablets of the Kouyûnjik Collection*, Vol. V., London, 1899, p. xviii*ff.*; and King, *Supplement*, London, 1914, p. xviii*ff.*

Astrological Omens concerning cities.

## TABLET WITH COLOPHON.

### TABLET FROM THE TEMPLE OF NEBO WITH COLOPHON.

[K. 7000]

Forecasts which formed the Fourth Tablet of the Series ⋈ ⟨⟨- 𒐼.

1854-5, and their examination by Rawlinson and Norris began very soon after. Mr. Bowler, a skilful draughtsman and copyist of tablets, whom Rawlinson employed in making transfers of copies of cuneiform texts for publication by lithography, rejoined a considerable number of fragments of bilingual lists, syllabaries, etc., which were published in the second volume of the *Cuneiform Inscriptions of Western Asia*, in 1866. In that year the Trustees of the British Museum employed George Smith to assist Rawlinson in sorting, classifying and rejoining fragments, and a comprehensive examination of the collection by him began. His personal interest in Assyriology was centred upon historical texts, especially those which threw any light on the Bible Narrative. But in the course of his search for stories of the campaigns of Sargon II, Sennacherib, Esarhaddon and Ashur-bani-pal, he discovered among other important documents (1) a series of portions of tablets which give the adventures of Gilgamish, an ancient king of Erech; (2) An account of the Deluge, which is supplied by the Eleventh Tablet of the Legend of Gilgamish (in more than one version); (3) A detailed description of the Creation; (4) the Legend of the Descent of Ishtar into Hades in quest of Tammuz. The general meaning of the texts was quite clear, but there were many gaps in them, and it was not until December, 1872, that George Smith published his description of the Legend of Gilgamish, and a translation of the "Chaldean Account of the Deluge." The interest which his paper evoked was universal, and the proprietors of the "Daily Telegraph" advocated that Smith should be at once dispatched to Nineveh to search for the missing fragments of tablets which would fill up the gaps in his texts, and generously offered to contribute 1,000 guineas towards the cost of the excavations. The Trustees accepted the offer and gave six months' leave of absence to Smith, who left London in January, and arrived in Môṣul in March, 1873. In the following May he recovered from Ḳuyûnjik a fragment that contained "the greater portion of seventeen "lines of inscription belonging to the first column of the "Chaldean account of the Deluge, and fitting into the only "place where there was a serious blank in the story."[1] During

---

[1] Smith, *Assyrian Discoveries*, London, 1875, p. 97.

the excavations which Smith carried out at Kuyûnjik in 1873 and 1874 he recovered many fragments of tablets, the texts of which enabled him to complete his description of the contents of the Twelve Tablets of the Legend of Gilgamish which included his translation of the story of the Deluge. Unfortunately Smith died of hunger and sickness near Aleppo in 1876, and he was unable to revise his early work, and to supplement it with the information which he had acquired during his latest travels in Assyria and Babylonia. Thanks to the excavations which were carried on at Kuyûnjik by the Trustees of the British Museum after his untimely death, several hundreds of tablets and fragments have been recovered, and many of these have been rejoined to the tablets of the older collection. By the careful study and investigation of the old and new material Assyriologists have, during the last forty years, been enabled to restore and complete many passages in the Legends of Gilgamish and the Flood. It is now clear that the Legend of the Flood had not originally any connection with the Legend of Gilgamish, and that it was introduced into it by a late editor or redactor of the Legend, probably in order to complete the number of the Twelve Tablets on which it was written in the time of Ashur-bani-pal.

### The Legend of the Deluge in Babylonia.

In the introduction to his paper on the "Chaldean Account of the Deluge," which Smith read in December, 1872, and published in 1873, he stated that the Assyrian text which he had found on Ashur-bani-pal's tablets was copied from an archetype at Erech in Lower Babylonia. This archetype was, he thought, "either written in, or translated into Semitic Babylonian, "at a very early period," and although he could not assign a date to it, he adduced a number of convincing proofs in support of his opinion. The language in which he assumed the Legend to have been originally composed was known to him under the name of "Accadian," or "Akkadian," but is now called "Sumerian." Recent research has shown that his view on this point was correct on the whole. But there is satisfactory proof available to show that versions or recensions of the Legend of the Deluge and of the Epic of Gilgamish existed both in Sumerian and Babylonian, as early as B.C. 2000. The discovery has been made of a fragment of a tablet with a small portion of the Babylonian version of the Legend of the Deluge inscribed upon it, and dated in a year which is the equivalent of the 11th year of Ammisaduga, *i.e.* about B.C. 2000.[1] And in the Museum at Philadelphia[2] is preserved half of a tablet which when whole contained a complete copy of the Sumerian version of the Legend, and must have been written about the same date. The fragment of the tablet written in the reign of Ammisaduga is of special importance because the colophon shows that the tablet to which it belonged was the second of a series, and that this series was not that of the Epic of Gilgamish, and from this we learn that in B.C. 2000 the Legend of the Deluge did not form the XIth Tablet of the Epic of Gilgamish, as it did in the reign of Ashur-bani-pal, or earlier. The Sumerian version is equally important, though from another point of view, for the contents and position of the portion of it that remains on the half of the tablet mentioned above make it certain that already at this early period there were several versions of the Legend of the Deluge current in the Sumerian language. The fact is that the Legend of the Deluge was then already so old in Mesopotamia that the scribes added to or abbreviated the text at will, and treated the incidents recorded in it according to local or popular taste, tradition and prejudice. There seems to be no evidence that proves conclusively that the Sumerian version is older than the Semitic, or that the latter was translated direct from the former version. It is probable that both the Sumerians and the Semites, each in their own way, attempted to commemorate an appalling disaster of unparalleled magnitude, the knowledge of which, through tradition, was common to both peoples. It is, at all events, clear that the Sumerians regarded the Deluge as an historic event, which they were, practically, able to date, for some of their tablets contain lists of kings who reigned before the Deluge, though it must be confessed that the lengths assigned to their reigns are incredible.

---

[1] Published by Scheil in Maspero's *Recueil*, Vol. XX, p. 55*ff*.

[2] The text is published by A. Poebel with transcription, commentary, etc., in *Historical Texts*, Philadelphia, 1914, and *Historical and Grammatical Texts*, Philadelphia, 1914.

It is not too much to assume that the original event commemorated in the Legend of the Deluge was a serious and prolonged inundation or flood in Lower Babylonia, which was accompanied by great loss of life and destruction of property. The Babylonian versions state that this inundation or flood was caused by rain, but passages in some of them suggest that the effects of the rainstorm were intensified by other physical happenings connected with the earth, of a most destructive character. The Hebrews also, as we may see from the Bible, had alternative views as to the cause of the Deluge. According to one, rain fell upon the earth for forty days and forty nights (Gen. vii, 12), and according to the other the Deluge came because " all the fountains of the " great deep " were broken up, and " the flood-gates of heaven were opened " (Gen. vii, 11). The latter view suggests that the rain flood was joined by the waters of the sea. Later tradition, based partly on Babylonian and partly on Hebrew sources, asserts in the " Cave of Treasures "[1] that when Noah had entered the Ark and the door was shut, " the sluices of heaven " were opened, and the deeps were rent asunder," and " that " the Ocean, that great sea that surroundeth the whole world, " vomited its waters, and the sluices of heaven being opened, " and the deeps of the earth being rent asunder, the store- " houses of the winds were opened, and the whirlwinds broke " loose, and the Ocean roared and poured out its waters in " floods." The ark was steered over the waters by an angel who acted as pilot, and when that had come to rest on the mountains of Ḳardô (Armenia) " God commanded the waters " and they separated from each other. The waters that " had been above ascended to their place above the heavens, " whence they had come ; and the waters that had come up " from under the earth returned to the lower deep ; and " the waters that were from the Ocean returned into it " (Brit. Mus. MS. Orient. No. 25,875, fol. 17b, col. 1 and fol. 18a, cols. 1 and 2). Many authorities seeking to find a foundation of fact for the Legend of the Deluge in Mesopotamia have assumed that the rain flood was accompanied either by an earthquake or a tidal wave, or by both. There is no doubt

---

[1] A famous work composed by members of the College of Edessa in the fifth or sixth century A.D.

that the cities of Lower Babylonia were nearer the sea in the Sumerian Period than they are at the present time, and it is a generally accepted view that the head of the Persian Gulf lay further to the north at that time. A cyclone coupled with a tidal wave is a sufficient base for any of the forms of the Legend now known.

A comparison of the contents of the various Sumerian and Babylonian versions of the Deluge that have come down to us shows us that they are incomplete. And as none of them tells so connected and full a narrative of the prehistoric shipbuilder as Berosus, a priest of Bêl, the great god of Babylon, it seems that the Mesopotamian scribes were content to copy the Legend in an abbreviated form. Berosus, it is true, is not a very ancient authority, for he was not born until the reign of Alexander the Great, but he was a learned man and was well acquainted with the Babylonian language, and with the ancient literature of his country, and he wrote a history of Babylonia, some fragments of which have been preserved to us in the works of Alexander Polyhistor, Eusebius, and others. The following is a version of the fragment which describes the flood that took place in the days of Xisuthrus, the tenth King of the Chaldeans, and is of importance for comparison with the rendering of the Legend of the Deluge, as found on the Ninevite tablets, which follows immediately after.

### The Legend of the Deluge According to Berosus.

"After the death of Ardates, his son Xisuthrus reigned
"eighteen *sari*. In his time happened a great Deluge; the
"history of which is thus described. The Deity, Cronus,
"appeared to him in a vision, and warned him that upon the
"15th day of the month Daesius there would be a flood, by
"which mankind would be destroyed. He therefore enjoined
"him to write a history of the beginning, procedure and
"conclusion of all things; and to bury it in the city of the
"Sun at Sippara; and to build a vessel, and take with him
"into it his friends and relations; and to convey on board
"everything necessary to sustain life, together with all the
"different animals, both birds and quadrupeds, and trust

## LEGEND OF DELUGE ACCORDING TO BEROSUS.

"himself fearlessly to the deep. Having asked the Deity, "whither he was to sail? he was answered, 'To the Gods': "upon which he offered up a prayer for the good of mankind. "He then obeyed the divine admonition; and built a vessel "5 stadia in length, and 2 in breadth. Into this he put "everything which he had prepared; and last of all con-"veyed into it his wife, his children, and his friends. After "the flood had been upon the earth, and was in time abated, "Xisuthrus sent out birds from the vessel; which, not finding "any food nor any place whereupon they might rest their "feet, returned to him again. After an interval of some "days, he sent them forth a second time; and they now re-"turned with their feet tinged with mud. He made a trial "a third time with these birds; but they returned to him no "more: from whence he judged that the surface of the earth "had appeared above the waters. He therefore made an "opening in the vessel, and upon looking out found that it "was stranded upon the side of some mountain; upon which "he immediately quitted it with his wife, his daughter, and "the pilot. Xisuthrus then paid his adoration to the earth, "and, having constructed an altar, offered sacrifices to the "gods, and, with those who had come out of the vessel with "him, disappeared. They, who remained within, finding that "their companions did not return, quitted the vessel with "many lamentations, and called continually on the name of "Xisuthrus. Him they saw no more; but they could dis-"tinguish his voice in the air, and could hear him admonish "them to pay due regard to religion; and likewise informed "them that it was upon account of his piety that he was "translated to live with the gods; that his wife and daughter, "and the pilot, had obtained the same honour. To this he "added that they should return to Babylonia; and, it was "ordained, search for the writings at Sippara, which they "were to make known to mankind: moreover that the place, "wherein they then were, was the land of Armenia. The "rest having heard these words, offered sacrifices to the gods; "and taking a circuit journeyed towards Babylonia." (Cory, *Ancient Fragments*, London, 1832, p. 26ff.)

## THE BABYLONIAN LEGEND OF THE DELUGE AS TOLD TO THE HERO GILGAMISH BY HIS ANCESTOR UTA-NAPISHTIM, WHO HAD BEEN MADE IMMORTAL BY THE GODS.

The form of the Legend of the Deluge given below is that which is found on the Eleventh of the Series of Twelve Tablets in the Library of Nebo at Nineveh, which described the life and exploits of Gilgamish (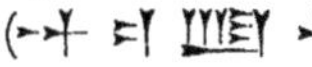), an early king of the city of Erech. As we have seen above, the Legend of the Deluge has in reality no connection with the Epic of Gilgamish, but was introduced into it by the editors of the Epic at a comparatively late period, perhaps even during the reign of Ashur-bani-pal (B.C. 668—626). A summary of the contents of the other Tablets of the Gilgamish Series is given in the following section of this short monograph. It is therefore only necessary to state here that Gilgamish, who was horrified and almost beside himself when his bosom friend and companion Enkidu (, Eabâni) died, meditated deeply how he could escape death himself. He knew that his ancestor Uta-Napishtim () had become immortal, therefore he determined to set out for the place where Uta-Napishtim lived so that he might obtain from him the secret of immortality. Guided by a dream in which he saw the direction of the place where Uta-Napishtim lived, Gilgamish set out for the Mountain of the Sunset, and, after great toil and many difficulties, came to the shore of a vast sea. Here he met Ur-Shanabi (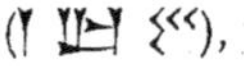), the boatman of Uta-Napishtim, who was persuaded to carry him in his boat over the "waters "of death" (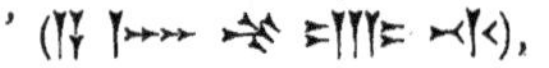), and at length he landed on the shore of the country of Uta-Napishtim. The immortal came down to the shore and asked the newcomer the object of his visit, and Gilgamish told him of the death of his great friend Enkidu, and of his desire to escape from death and to find immortality. Uta-Napishtim having made to Gilgamish some remarks which seem to indicate that in his opinion death was inevitable,

## AS TOLD TO GILGAMISH BY UTA-NAPISHTIM.

1. Gilgamish[1] said unto Uta-Napishtim, to Uta-Napishtim the remote:
2. "I am looking at thee, Uta-Napishtim.
3. "Thy person is not altered; even as am I so art thou.
4. "Verily, nothing about thee is changed; even as am I so art thou.
5. "[Moved is my] heart to do battle,
6. "But thou art at leisure and dost lie upon thy back.
7. "How then wast thou able to enter the company of the gods and see life?"

Thereupon Uta-Napishtim related to Gilgamish the Story of the Deluge, and the Eleventh Tablet continues thus :—

8. Uta-Napishtim said unto him, to Gilgamish:
9. "I will reveal unto thee, O Gilgamish, a hidden mystery,
10. "And a secret matter of the gods I will declare unto thee.
11. "Shurippak,[2] a city which thou thyself knowest,
12. "On [the bank] of the river Puratti (Euphrates) is situated,
13. "That city was old and the gods [dwelling] within it—
14. "Their hearts induced the great gods to make a windstorm (𒀀𒁍𒁉, a-bu-bi),[3]
15. "Their father Anu (𒀭𒀭),
16. "Their counsellor, the warrior Enlil (𒀭𒂗𒆤),
17. "Their messenger En-urta (𒀭𒊩𒌆) [and]
18. "Their prince Ennugi (𒀭𒂗𒉬).
19. "Nin-igi-azag, Ea, was with them [in council] and
20. "reported their word to the house of reeds.

[FIRST SPEECH OF EA TO UTA-NAPISHTIM WHO IS SLEEPING IN A REED HUT.]

21. "O House of reeds, O House of reeds! O Wall, O Wall!

---

[1] A transcript of the cuneiform text by George Smith, who was the first to translate it, will be found in Rawlinson, *Cuneiform Inscriptions of Western Asia*, Vol. IV., plates 43 and 44; and a transcript, with transliteration and translation by the late Prof. L. W. King, is given in his *First Steps in Assyrian*, London, 1898, p. 161*ff*.

[2] The site of this very ancient city is marked by the mounds of Fârah, near the Shaṭṭ al-Kâr, which is probably the old bed of the river Euphrates; many antiquities belonging to the earliest period of the rule of the Sumerians have been found there.

[3] Like the *habûb* of modern times, a sort of cyclone.

The Eleventh Tablet of the Gilgamish Series containing the Story of the Deluge as told to Gilgamish by his deified ancestor Uta-Napishtim, an antediluvian king of Erech. A portion of one end of the tablets was vitrified when Ashur-bani-pal's palace and the Library of Nebo were destroyed by fire. From the Library of the Temple of Nebo. Size, seven-eighths of the original. K. 3321 + S. 1881.

22. "O House of reeds, hear! O Wall, understand!
23. "O man of Shurippak, son of Ubara-Tutu
       (𒑰 𒂊𒐊 𒈨𒐊 𒂊𒐊 𒂊𒐊),
24. "Throw down the house, build a ship,
25. "Forsake wealth, seek after life,
26. "Abandon possessions, save thy life,
27. "Carry grain of every kind into the ship.
28. "The ship which thou shalt build,
29. "The dimensions thereof shall be measured,
30. "The breadth and the length thereof shall be the same.
31. ". . . the ocean, provide it with a roof."

[UTA-NAPISHTIM'S ANSWER TO EA.]

32. "I understood and I said unto Ea, my lord:
33. "[I comprehend] my lord, that which thou hast ordered,
34. "I will regard it with great reverence, and will perform it.
35. "But what shall I say to the town, to the multitude, and to the elders?"

[SECOND SPEECH OF EA.]

36. "Ea opened his mouth and spake
37. "And said unto his servant, myself,
38. ". . . Thus shalt thou say unto them:
39. "Ill-will hath the god Enlil formed against me,
40. "Therefore I can no longer dwell in your city,
41. "And never more will I turn my countenance upon the soil of Enlil.
42. "I will descend into the ocean to dwell with my lord Ea.
43. "But upon you he will rain riches:
44. "A catch of birds, a catch of fish
45. ". . . an [abundant] harvest,
46. ". . . the prince (?) of the darkness
47. ". . . shall make a violent cyclone [to fall upon you].

[THE BUILDING OF THE SHIP.]

48. "As soon as [the dawn] broke . . .
       [Lines 49–54 broken away.]
55. "The weak [man] . . . brought bitumen,
56. "The strong [man] . . . brought what was needed.

## 34 THE BABYLONIAN LEGEND OF THE DELUGE

57. " On the fifth day I decided upon its plan.
58. " According to the plan its walls were 10 *Gar* (*i.e.* 120 cubits) high,
59. " And the circuit of the roof thereof was equally 10 *Gar*.
60. " I measured out the hull thereof and marked it out (?)
61. " I covered (?) it six times.
62. " Its exterior I divided into seven,
63. " Its interior I divided into nine,
64. " Water bolts I drove into the middle of it.
65. " I provided a steering pole, and fixed what was needful for it,
66. " Six *sar* of bitumen I poured over the inside wall,
67. " Three *sar* of pitch I poured into the inside.
68. " The men who bear loads brought three *sar* of oil,
69. " Besides a *sar* of oil which the offering consumed,
70. " And two *sar* of oil which the boatman hid.
71. " I slaughtered oxen for the [work]people,
72. " I slew sheep every day.
73. " Beer, sesame wine, oil and wine
74. " I made the people drink as if they were water from the river.
75. " I celebrated a feast-day as if it had been New Year's Day.
76. " I opened [a box of ointment], I laid my hands in unguent.
77. " Before the sunset the ship was finished.
78. " [Since] . . . was difficult.
79. " The shipbuilders brought the . . . of the ship, above and below;
80. " . . . two-thirds of it.

[THE LOADING OF THE SHIP.]

81. " With everything that I possessed I loaded it (*i.e.* the ship)
82. " With everything that I possessed of silver I loaded it.
83. " With everything that I possessed of gold I loaded it.
84. " With all that I possessed of living grain I loaded it.
85. " I made to go up into the ship all my family and kinsfolk,

86. "The cattle of the field, the beasts of the field, all handicraftsmen I made them go up into it.
87. "The god Shamash had appointed me a time (saying)
88. "The Power of Darkness will at eventide make a rain-flood to fall;
89. "Then enter into the ship and shut thy door.
90. "The appointed time drew nigh;
91. "The Power of Darkness made a rain-flood to fall at eventide.
92. "I watched the coming of the [approaching] storm,
93. "When I saw it terror possessed me,
94. "I went into the ship and shut my door.
95. "To the pilot of the ship, Puzur-Bêl (or Puzur-Amurri 𒄑 𒂗 𒆤 𒅆 𒀭 𒂊) the sailor
96. "I committed the great house (*i.e.* ship), together with the contents thereof.

[THE ABUBU (CYCLONE) AND ITS EFFECTS DESCRIBED.]

97. "As soon as the gleam of dawn shone in the sky
98. "A black cloud from the foundation of heaven came up.
99. "Inside it the god Adad (Rammânu) thundered,
100. "The gods Nabû and Sharru (*i.e.* Marduk) went before,
101. "Marching as messengers over high land and plain,
102. "Irragal (Nergal) tore out the post of the ship,
103. "En-urta (Ninib) went on, he made the storm to descend.
104. "The Anunnaki[1] brandished their torches,
105. "With their glare they lighted up the land.
106. "The whirlwind (or, cyclone) of Adad swept up to heaven.
107. "Every gleam of light was turned into darkness.
108. "..... the land ...... as if ...... had laid it waste.
109. "A whole day long [the flood descended] . . .
110. "Swiftly it mounted up . . . . . [the water] reached to the mountains
111. "[The water] attacked the people like a battle.
112. "Brother saw not brother.

---

[1] The star-gods of the southern sky.

113. "Men could not be known (or, recognized) in heaven.
114. "The gods were terrified at the cyclone.
115. "They betook themselves to flight and went up into the heaven of Anu.
116. "The gods crouched like a dog and cowered by the wall.
117. "The goddess Ishtar cried out like a woman in travail.
118. "The Lady of the Gods lamented with a loud voice [saying]:

[ISHTAR'S LAMENT.]

119. "Verily the former dispensation is turned into mud,
120. "Because I commanded evil among the company of the gods.
121. "When I commanded evil among the company of the gods,
122. "I commanded battle for the destruction of my people.
123. "Did I of myself bring forth my people
124. "That they might fill the sea like little fishes?"

[UTA-NAPISHTIM'S STORY CONTINUED.]

125. "The gods of the Anunnaki wailed with her.
126. "The gods bowed themselves, and sat down, and wept.
127. "Their lips were shut tight (in distress) . . .
128. "For six days and nights
129. "The storm raged, and the cyclone overwhelmed the land.

[THE ABATING OF THE STORM.]

130. "When the seventh day approached the cyclone and the raging flood ceased:
131. "—now it had fought like an army.
132. "The sea became quiet and went down, and the cyclone and the rain-storm ceased.
133. "I looked over the sea and a calm had come,
134. "And all mankind were turned into mud,
135. "The land had been laid flat like a terrace.
136. "I opened the air-hole and the light fell upon my face,
137. "I bowed myself, I sat down, I cried,
138. "My tears poured down over my cheeks.

139. " I looked over the quarters of the world—open sea !
140. " After twelve days an island appeared.
141. " The ship took its course to the land of Niṣir (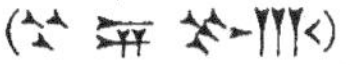)
142. " The mountain of Niṣir held the ship, it let it not move.
143. " The first day, the second day, the mountain of Niṣir held the ship and let it not move.
144. " The third day, the fourth day, the mountain of Niṣir held the ship and let it not move.
145. " The fifth day, the sixth day, the mountain of Niṣir held the ship and let it not move.
146. " When the seventh day had come
147. " I brought out a dove and let her go free.
148. " The dove flew away and [then] came back;
149. " Because she had no place to alight on she came back.
150. " I brought out a swallow and let her go free.
151. " The swallow flew away and [then] came back;
152. " Because she had no place to alight on she came back.
153. " I brought out a raven and let her go free.
154. " The raven flew away, she saw the sinking waters.
155. " She ate, she pecked in the ground, she croaked, she came not back.

[Uta-Napishtim leaves the Ship.]

156. " Then I brought out everything to the four winds and offered up a sacrifice ;
157. " I poured out a libation on the peak of the mountain.
158. " Seven by seven I set out the vessels,
159. " Under them I piled reeds, cedarwood and myrtle (?).
160. " The gods smelt the savour,
161. " The gods smelt the sweet savour.
162. " The gods gathered together like flies over him that sacrificed.

[Speech of Ishtar, Lady of the Gods.]

163. " Now when the Lady of the Gods came nigh,
164. " She lifted up the priceless jewels which Anu had made according to her desire, [saying]
165. " O ye gods here present, as I shall never forget the lapis-lazuli jewels of my neck

## THE ELEVENTH TABLET OF THE GILGAMISH SERIES
(lines 165-214).

Portion of another copy of the Story of the Deluge, from a tablet which probably belonged to the Palace Library of Ashur-bani-pal at Nineveh. Photograph one-seventh larger than the original. K. 3375.

## THE LEGEND AS TOLD BY UTA-NAPISHTIM.

166. "So shall I ever think about these days, and shall forget them nevermore!
167. "Let the gods come to the offering,
168. "But let not Enlil come to the offering,
169. "Because he would not accept counsel and made the cyclone,
170. "And delivered my people over to destruction."

[THE ANGER OF ENLIL (BÊL).]

171. "Now when Enlil came nigh
172. "He saw the ship; then was Enlil wroth
173. "And he was filled with anger against the gods, the Igigi [saying]:[1]
174. "What kind of a being hath escaped with his life?
175. "He shall not remain alive, a man among the destruction!"

[SPEECH OF EN-URTA.]

176. "Then En-Urta opened his mouth and spake
177. "And said unto the warrior Enlil (Bêl):
178. "Who besides the god Ea can make a plan?
179. "The god Ea knoweth everything.
180. "He opened his mouth and spake
181. "And said unto the warrior Enlil (Bêl),
182. "O Prince among the gods, thou warrior,
183. "How couldst thou, not accepting counsel, make a cyclone?
184. "He who is sinful, on him lay his sin,
185. "He who transgresseth, on him lay his transgression.
186. "But be merciful that [everything] be not destroyed; be long-suffering that [man be not blotted out].
187. "Instead of thy making a cyclone,
188. "Would that a lion had come and diminished mankind.
189. "Instead of thy making a cyclone
190. "Would that a wolf had come and diminished mankind.
191. "Instead of thy making a cyclone

[1] The star-gods of the northern heaven.

192. "Would that a famine had arisen and [laid waste] the land.
193. "Instead of thy making a cyclone
194. "Would that Urra (𒀭, the Plague god) had risen up and [laid waste] the land.
195. "As for me I have not revealed the secret of the great gods.
196. "I made Atra-ḫasis (𒁹 𒂊 𒄩 𒋀) to see a vision, and thus he heard the secret of the gods.
197. "Now therefore counsel him with counsel."

[EA DEIFIES UTA-NAPISHTIM AND HIS WIFE.]

198. "Then the god Ea went up into the ship,
199. "He seized me by the hand and brought me forth.
200. "He brought forth my wife and made her to kneel by my side.
201. "He turned our faces towards each other, he stood between us, he blessed us [saying],
202. "Formerly Uta-Napishtim was a man merely,
203. "But now let Uta-Napishtim and his wife be like unto the gods, ourselves.
204. "Uta-Napishtim shall dwell afar off, at the mouth of the rivers."

[UTA-NAPISHTIM ENDS HIS STORY OF THE DELUGE.]

205. "And they took me away to a place afar off, and made me to dwell at the mouth of the rivers."

The contents of the remainder of the text on the Eleventh Tablet of the Gilgamish Series are described on p. 54.

### THE EPIC OF GILGAMISH.[1]

The narrative of the life, exploits and travels of Gilgamish, king of Erech, filled Twelve Tablets which formed the Series called from the first three words of the First Tablet, SHA NAGBU IMURU, *i.e.*, "He who hath seen all things." The exact period of the reign of this king is unknown, but there is

---

[1] The name of Gilgamish was formerly read "Izdubar," "Gizdubar," or "Gishdubar." He is probably referred to as Γίλγαμος in Aelian, *De Natura Animalium*, XII, 21 (ed. Didot, Paris, 1858, p. 210).

no doubt that he lived and ruled at Erech before the conquest of Mesopotamia by the Semites. According to a tablet from Niffar he was the fifth of a line of Sumerian rulers at Erech, and he reigned 126 years; his name is said to mean " The Fire-god is a commander."[1] The principal authorities for the Epic are the numerous fragments of the tablets that were found in the ruins of the Library of Nebo and the Royal Library of Ashur-bani-pal at Nineveh, and are now in the British Museum.[2] The contents of the Twelve Tablets may be briefly described thus :

### First Tablet.

The opening lines describe the great knowledge and wisdom of Gilgamish, who saw everything, learned everything, understood everything, who probed to the bottom the hidden mysteries of wisdom, and who knew the history of everything that happened before the Deluge. He travelled far over sea and land, and performed mighty deeds, and then he cut upon a tablet of stone an account of all that he had done and suffered. He built the wall of Erech, founded the holy temple of E-Anna, and carried out other great architectural works. He was a semi-divine being, for his body was formed of the " flesh of the gods " 𒄊𒅔 𒁹, and " Two-thirds of him were god, and one-third was man " 𒐻 𒐼 𒁹 𒅔 𒁹 𒐖 𒂊 𒐼 𒀭 𒅔 𒐎 𒁹 (l. 51). The description of his person is lost. As Shepherd (*i.e.*, King) of Erech he forced the people to toil overmuch, and his demands reduced them to such a state of misery that they cried out to the gods and begged them to create some king who should control Gilgamish and give them deliverance from him. The gods hearkened to the prayer of the men of Erech, and they commanded the goddess Aruru to create a rival to Gilgamish. The goddess agreed to do their bidding, and having planned in her mind what manner of being she intended to make, she washed her hands, took a piece of clay and spat upon it, and made a male creature like the god Anu. His body was covered all

---

Langdon, *Epic of Gilgamish*, pp. 207, 208.

[2] The greater number of these have been collected, grouped and published by Haupt, *Das Babylonische Nimrodepos*, Leipzig, 1884 and 1891 ; and see his work on the Twelfth Tablet in *Beiträge zur Assyriologie*, Vol. I, p. 49*ff.*

over with hair. The hair of his head was long like that of a woman, and he wore clothing like that of Gira (or, Sumuggan), a goddess of vegetation, *i.e.*, he appeared to be clothed with leaves. He was different in every way from the people of the country, and his name was Enkidu (Eabani). He lived in the forests on the hills, ate herbs like the gazelle, drank with the wild cattle, and herded with the beasts of the field. He was mighty in stature, invincible in strength, and obtained complete mastery over all the creatures of the forests in which he lived.

One day a certain hunter went out to snare game, and he dug pit-traps and laid nets, and made his usual preparations for roping in his prey. But after doing this for three days he found that his pits were filled up and his nets smashed, and he saw Enkidu releasing the beasts that had been snared. The hunter was terrified at the sight of Enkidu, and went home hastily and told his father what he had seen and how badly he had fared. By his father's advice he went to Erech, and reported to Gilgamish what had happened. When Gilgamish heard his story he advised him to act upon a suggestion which the hunter's father had already made, namely that he should hire a harlot and take her out to the forest, so that Enkidu might be ensnared by the sight of her beauty, and take up his abode with her. The hunter accepted this advice, and having found a harlot to help him in removing Enkidu from the forests (thus enabling him to gain a living), he set out from Erech with her and in due course arrived at the forest where Enkidu lived, and sat down by the place where the beasts came to drink.

On the second day when the beasts came to drink and Enkidu was with them, the woman carried out the instructions which the hunter had given her, and when Enkidu saw her cast aside her veil, he left his beasts and came to her, and remained with her for six days and seven nights. At the end of this period he returned to the beasts with which he had lived on friendly terms, but as soon as the gazelle winded him they took to flight, and the wild cattle disappeared into the woods. When Enkidu saw the beasts forsake him his knees gave way, and he swooned from sheer shame; but when he came to himself he returned to the harlot. She spoke to him flattering words, and asked him why he wandered with the wild beasts in the desert, and then told him she wished to take him back with her to Erech, where Anu and Ishtar lived, and where the mighty Gilgamish reigned. Enkidu hearkened and finally went back with her to her city, where she described the wisdom, power and might of Gilgamish, and took steps to make Enkidu known to him. But before Enkidu arrived, Gilgamish had been warned of his existence and coming in two dreams which he related to his mother Ninsunna (𒀭 𒊩𒌆 𒄢 𒈾), and when he and Enkidu learned to know each other subsequently, these two mighty heroes became great friends.

### Second Tablet.

When Enkidu came to Erech the habits of the people of the city were strange to him, but under the tuition of the harlot he learned to eat bread and to drink beer, and to wear clothes, and he anointed his body with unguents. He went out into the forests with his hunting implements and snared the gazelle and slew the panther, and obtained animals for sacrifice, and gained reputation as a mighty hunter and as a good shepherd. In due course he attracted the notice of Gilgamish, who did not, however, like his uncouth appearance and ways, but after a time, when the citizens of Erech praised him and admired his strong and vigorous stature, he made friends with him and rejoiced in him, and planned an expedition with him. Before they set out, Gilgamish wished to pay a visit to the goddess Ishkhara (𒀭 𒈦 𒄩 𒊏), but Enkidu, fearing that the influence of the goddess would have a bad effect upon his friend, urged him to abandon the visit. This Gilgamish refused to do, and when Enkidu declared that by force he would prevent him going to the goddess, a violent quarrel broke out between the two heroes, and they appealed to arms. After a fierce fight Enkidu conquered Gilgamish, who apparently abandoned his visit to the goddess. The text of the Second Tablet is very much mutilated, and the authorities on the subject are not agreed as to the exact placing of the fragments. The above details are derived from a tablet at Philadelphia.[1]

---

[1] See Langdon, *The Epic of Gilgamish*, Philadelphia, 1917.

## The Third Tablet.

The correct order of the fragments of this Tablet has not yet been ascertained, but among the contents of the first part of its text a lament by Enkidu that he was associated with the harlot seems to have had a place. Whether he had left the city of Erech and gone back to his native forest is not clear, but the god Shamash, having heard his cursing of the harlot, cried to him from heaven, saying, " Why, O Enkidu, " dost thou curse the temple woman ? She gave thee food to " eat which was meet only for a god, she gave thee wine to " drink which was meet only for a king, she arrayed thee in " splendid apparel, and made thee to possess as thy friend " the noble Gilgamish. And at present Gilgamish is thy " bosom friend. He maketh thee to lie down on a large couch, " and to sleep in a good, well-decked bed, and to occupy the " chair of peace, the chair on the left-hand side. The princes " of the earth kiss thy feet. He maketh the people of Erech " to sigh for thee, and many folk to cry out for thee, and to " serve thee. And for thy sake he putteth on coarse attire " and arrayeth himself in the skin of the lion, and pursueth " thee over the plain." When Enkidu heard these words his anxious heart had peace.

To the Third Tablet probably belongs the fragment in which Enkidu relates to Gilgamish a horrifying dream which he had had. In his dream it seemed to him that there were thunderings in heaven and quaking upon earth, and a being with an awful visage, and nails like an eagle's talons, gripped him and carried him off and forced him to go down into the dark abyss of the dread goddess, Irkalla. From this abode he who once " went in never came out, and he who travelled " along that road never returned. He who dwelleth there is " without light, the beings therein eat dust and feed upon " mud ; they are clad in feathers and have wings like birds, " they see no light, and they live in the darkness of night." Here Enkidu saw in his dream creatures who had been kings when they lived upon the earth, and shadowy beings offering roasted meat to Anu and Enlil, and cool drinks poured out from waterskins. In this House of Dust dwelt high priests, ministrants, the magician and the prophet, and the deities Etana, Sumukan, Eresh-kigal, Queen of the Earth, and Bêlit-ṣêri, who registered the deeds done upon the earth.

When Gilgamish heard this dream, he brought out a table, and setting on it honey and butter placed it before Shamash.

### The Fourth Tablet.

Gilgamish then turned to Enkidu and invited him to go with him to the temple of Nin-Makh to see the servant of his mother, Ninsunna, in order to consult her as to the meaning of the dream. They went there, and Enkidu told his dream, and the wise woman offered up incense and asked Shamash why he had given to her son a heart which could never keep still. She next referred to the perilous expedition against the mighty King Khumbaba, which he had decided to undertake with Enkidu, and apparently hoped that the god would prevent her son from leaving Erech. But Gilgamish was determined to march against Khumbaba, and he and Enkidu set out without delay for the mountains where grew the cedars.

### The Fifth Tablet.

In due course the two heroes reached the forest of cedars, and they contemplated with awe their great height and their dense foliage. The cedars were under the special protection of Bêl, who had appointed to be their keeper Khumbaba, a being whose voice was like the roar of a storm, whose mouth was like that of the gods, and whose breath was like a gale of wind. When Enkidu saw how dense was the forest and how threatening, he tried to make Gilgamish turn back, but all his entreaties were in vain. As they were going through the forest to attack Khumbaba, Enkidu dreamed two or three dreams, and when he related them to Gilgamish, this hero interpreted them as auguries of their success and the slaughter of Khumbaba. The fragmentary character of the text here makes it very difficult to find out exactly what steps the two heroes took to overcome Khumbaba, but there is no doubt that they did overcome him, and that they returned to Erech in triumph.

## The Sixth Tablet

On his return to Erech, Gilgamish

1. Washed his armour, cleaned his weapons,
2. Dressed his hair and let it fall down on his back.
3. He cast off his dirty garments and put on clean ones.
4. He arrayed himself in the [royal head-cloth], he bound on the fillet,
5. He put on his crown, he bound on the fillet.
6. Then the eyes of the Majesty of the goddess Ishtar lighted on the goodliness of Gilgamish [and she said],
7. "Go to, Gilgamish, thou shalt be my lover.
8. "Give me thy [love]-fruit, give to me, I say.
9. "Thou shalt be my man, I will be thy woman.
10. "I will make to be harnessed for thee a chariot of lapis-lazuli and gold.
11. "The wheels thereof shall be of gold and the horns of precious stones.
12. "Thou shalt harness daily to it mighty horses.
13. "Come into our house with the perfume of the cedar upon thee.
14. "When thou enterest into our house
15. "Those who sit upon thrones shall kiss thy feet.
16. "Kings, lords and nobles shall bow their backs before thee.
17. "The gifts of mountain and land they shall bring as tribute to thee.
18. "Thy . . . and thy sheep shall bring forth twins.
19. "Baggage animals shall come laden with tribute.
20. "The [horse] in thy chariot shall prance proudly,
21. "There shall be none like unto the beast that is under thy yoke."

In answer to Ishtar's invitation Gilgamish makes a long speech, in which he reviews the calamities and misfortunes of those who have been unfortunate enough to become the lovers of the goddess. Her love is like a door that lets in wind and storm, a fortress that destroys the warriors inside it, an elephant that smashes his howdah, etc. He says, " What " lover didst thou love for long ? Which of thy shepherds

## THE SIXTH TABLET. 47

"flourished? Come now, I will describe the calamity [that "goeth with thee]." He refers to Tammuz, the lover of her youth, for whom year by year she arranges wailing commemorations. Every creature that falls under her sway suffers mutilation or death, the bird's wings are broken, the lion is destroyed, the horse is driven to death with whip and spur; and his speech concludes with the words: "Dost thou love "me, and wouldst "thou treat me "as thou didst "them?"

When Ishtar heard these words she was filled with rage, and she went up to heaven and complained to Anu, her father, and Antu, her mother, that Gilgamish had cursed her and revealed all her iniquitous deeds and actions.

Extract from the text of the Sixth Tablet of the Gilgamish Series (lines 50-70), containing a part of the speech which Gilgamish addressed to Ishtar in answer to her overtures to him. He reviles the goddess and reminds her of the death of Tammuz, and the sufferings of all the creatures that have been unfortunate enough to enter her service. From Rawlinson, *Cuneiform Inscriptions of Western Asia*, Vol. IV, Plate 41, col. 2. (K. 2589.)

She followed up her complaint with the request that Anu should create a mighty bull of heaven to destroy Gilgamish, and she threatened her father that if he did not grant her request she would do works of destruction, presumably in the world. Anu created the fire-breathing (?) bull of heaven and sent him to the city of Erech, where he destroyed large numbers of the people. At length Enkidu and Gilgamish determined to go forth and slay the bull. When they came to the place where he was, Enkidu seized him by the tail, and Gilgamish delivered deadly blows between his neck and his horns, and together they killed him. As soon as Ishtar heard of the death of the bull she rushed out on the battlements of the walls of Erech and cursed Gilgamish for destroying her bull. When Enkidu heard what Ishtar said, he went and tore off a portion of the bull's flesh from his right side, and threw it at the goddess, saying, "Could I but fight with thee I would serve thee " as I have served him! I would twine his entrails about thee." Then Ishtar gathered together all her temple women and harlots, and with them made lamentation over the portion of the bull which Enkidu had thrown at her.

And Gilgamish called together the artisans of Erech who came and marvelled at the size of the bull's horns, for their bulk was equal to 30 minas of lapis-lazuli, and their thickness to the length of two fingers, and they could contain six *Kur* measures of oil. Then Gilgamish took them to the temple of the god Lugalbanda and hung them up there on the throne of his majesty, and having made his offering he and Enkidu went to the Euphrates and washed their hands, and walked back to the market-place of Erech. As they went through the streets of the city the people thronged about them to get a sight of their faces. When Gilgamish asked:

" Who is splendid among men?
" Who is glorious among heroes?"

these questions were answered by the women of the palace who cried:

" Gilgamish is splendid among men.
" Gilgamish is glorious among heroes."

When Gilgamish entered his palace he ordered a great festival to be kept, and his guests were provided by him with beds to sleep on. On the night of the festival Enkidu had a dream, and he rose up and related it to Gilgamish.

### The Seventh Tablet.

About the contents of the Seventh Tablet there is considerable doubt, and the authorities differ in their opinions about them. A large number of lines of text are wanting at the beginning of the Tablet, but it is very probable that they contained a description of Enkidu's dream. This may have been followed by an interpretation of the dream, either by Gilgamish or some one else, but whether this be so or not, it seems tolerably certain that the dream portended disaster for Enkidu. A fragment, which seems to belong to this Tablet beyond doubt, describes the sickness and death of Enkidu. The cause of his sickness is unknown, and the fragment merely states that he took to his bed and lay there for ten days, when his illness took a turn for the worse, and on the twelfth day he died. He may have died of wounds received in some fight, but it is more probable that he succumbed to an attack of Mesopotamian fever. When Gilgamish was told that his brave friend and companion in many fights was dead, he could not believe it, and he thought that he must be asleep, but when he found that death had really carried off Enkidu, he broke out into the lament which formed the beginning of the text of the next Tablet.

### The Eighth Tablet.

In this lament he calls Enkidu his brave friend and the "panther of the desert," and refers to their hunts in the mountains, and to their slaughter of the bull of heaven, and to the overthrow of Khumbaba in the forest of cedar, and then he asks him:

"What kind of sleep is this which hath laid hold upon "thee?

"Thou starest out blankly (?) and hearest me not!"

But Enkidu moved not, and when Gilgamish touched his breast his heart was still. Then laying a covering over him as carefully as if he had been his bride, he turned away from the dead body and in his grief roared like a raging lion and like a lioness robbed of her whelps.

## The Ninth Tablet.

In bitter grief Gilgamish wandered about the country uttering lamentations for his beloved companion, Enkidu. As he went about he thought to himself,

"I myself shall die, and shall not I then be as Enkidu?
"Sorrow hath entered into my soul,
"Because of the fear of death which hath got hold of me do I wander over the country."

His fervent desire was to escape from death, and remembering that his ancestor Uta-Napishtim, the son of Ubara-Tutu, had become deified and immortal, Gilgamish determined to set out for the place where he lived in order to obtain from him the secret of immortality. Where Uta-Napishtim lived was unknown to Gilgamish, but he seems to have made up his mind that he would have to face danger in reaching the place, for he says, "I will set out and travel quickly. I shall reach the defiles in the mountains by night, and if I see lions, and am terrified at them, I shall lift up my head and appeal to the goddess Sin, and to Ishtar, the Lady of the Gods, who is wont to hearken to my prayers." After Gilgamish set out to go to the west he was attacked either by men or animals, but he overcame them and went on until he arrived at Mount Mashu, where it would seem the sun was thought both to rise and to set. The approach to this mountain was guarded by Scorpion-men, whose aspect was so terrible that the mere sight of it was sufficient to kill the mortal who beheld them; even the mountains collapsed under the glance of their eyes. When Gilgamish saw the Scorpion-men he was smitten with fear, and under the influence of his terror the colour of his face changed; but he plucked up courage and bowed to them humbly. Then a Scorpion-man cried out to his wife, saying, "The body of him that cometh to us is the flesh of the gods," and she replied, "Two-thirds of him is god, and the other third is man." The Scorpion-man then received Gilgamish kindly, and warned him that the way which he was about to travel was full of danger and difficulty. Gilgamish told him that he was in search of his ancestor, Uta-Napishtim, who had been deified and made immortal by the gods, and that it was his intention to go to him to learn the secret of immortality. The Scorpion-man in answer told him that it was impossible for him to continue his journey through that country, for no man had ever succeeded in passing through the dark region of that mountain, which required twelve double-hours to traverse. Nothing dismayed, Gilgamish set out on the road through the mountains, and the darkness increased in density every hour, but he struggled on, and at the end of the twelfth hour he arrived at a region where there was bright daylight, and he entered a lovely garden, filled with trees loaded with luscious fruits, and he saw the " tree of the gods."

## The Tenth Tablet.

In the region to which Gilgamish had come stood the palace or fortress of the goddess Siduri-Sabîtu, and to this he directed his steps with the view of obtaining help to continue his journey. The goddess wore a girdle and sat upon a throne by the side of the sea, and when she saw him coming towards her palace, travel-stained and clad in the ragged skin of some animal, she thought that he might prove an undesirable visitor and so ordered the door of her palace to be closed against him. But Gilgamish managed to obtain speech with her, and having asked her what ailed her, and why she had closed her door, he threatened to smash the bolt and break down the door. In answer Siduri-Sabîtu said to him:—

33. " Why are thy cheeks wasted ? Thy face is bowed down,
34. " Thine heart is sad, thy form is dejected.
35. " Why is there lamentation in thy heart ? "

And she went on to tell him that he had the appearance of one who had travelled far, that he was a painful sight to look upon, that his face was burnt, and finally seems to have suggested that he was a runaway trying to escape from the country. To this Gilgamish replied :

39. " Why should not my cheeks be wasted, my face bowed down,
40. " My heart sad, my form dejected ? "

And then he told the goddess that his ill-looks and miserable appearance were due to the fact that death had carried off his dear friend Enkidu, the " panther of the desert," who had traversed the mountains with him and had helped him to overcome Khumbaba in the cedar forest, and to slay the bull of heaven, Enkidu his dear friend who had fought with lions and killed them, and who had been with him in all his difficulties ; and, he added, " I wept over him for six days and nights . . . . before I would let him be buried." Continuing his narrative, Gilgamish said to Sabîtu-Siduri :

57. " I was horribly afraid . . .
58. " I was afraid of death, and therefore I fled through the country.
" The fate of my friend lieth heavily upon me,
59. " Therefore am I travelling on a long journey through the country.
" The fate of my friend lieth heavily upon me,
60. " Therefore am I travelling on a long journey through the country.
61. " How is it possible for me to keep silence about it ?
How is it possible for me to cry out [the story of] it ?
62. " My friend whom I loved hath become like the dust.
" Enkidu, my friend whom I loved hath become like the dust.
63. " Shall not I myself also be obliged to lay me down
64. " And never again rise up to all eternity ? "

65. Gilgamish [continued] to speak unto Sabîtu [saying] :
66. " [O] Sabîtu, which is the way to Uta-Napishtim ?
67. " What is the description thereof ? Give me, give me the description thereof.
68. " If it be possible I will cross the sea,
69. " If it be impossible I will travel by land."

70. Then Sabîtu answered and said unto Gilgamish :

71. "There is no passage most assuredly, O Gilgamish.
72. "And no one, from the earliest times, hath been able to cross the sea.
73. "The hero Shamash (the Sun-god) hath indeed crossed the sea, but who besides him could do so?
74. "The passage is hard, and the way is difficult.
75. "And the Waters of Death which block the other end of it are deep.
76. "How then, Gilgamish, wilt thou be able to cross the sea?
77. "When thou arrivest at the Waters of Death what wilt thou do?"

Sabîtu then told Gilgamish that Ur-Shanabi, the boatman of Uta-Napishtim, was in the place, and that he should see him, and added:

81. "If it be possible cross with him, and if it be impossible come back."

Gilgamish left the goddess and succeeded in finding Ur-Shanabi, the boatman, who addressed to him words similar to those of Sabîtu quoted above. Gilgamish answered him as he had answered Sabîtu, and then asked him for news about the road to Uta-Napishtim. In reply Ur-Shanabi told him to take his axe and to go down into the forest and cut a number of poles 60 cubits long; Gilgamish did so, and when he returned with them he went up into the boat with Ur-Shanabi, and they made a voyage of one month and fifteen days; on the third day they reached the [limit of the] Waters of Death, which Ur-Shanabi told Gilgamish not to touch with his hand. Meanwhile, Uta-Napishtim had seen the boat coming and, as something in its appearance seemed strange to him, he went down to the shore to see who the newcomers were. When he saw Gilgamish he asked him the same questions that Sabîtu and Ur-Shanabi had asked him, and Gilgamish answered as he had answered them, and then went on to tell him the reason for his coming. He said that he had determined to go to visit Uta-Napishtim, the remote, and had therefore journeyed far and that in the course of his travels he had passed over difficult mountains and crossed the sea. He had not succeeded in entering the house of Sabîtu, for she had caused him to be driven from her door on account of his dirty, ragged, and travel-stained apparel. He had eaten birds and beasts of many kinds, the lion, the panther, the jackal, the antelope, mountain goat, etc., and, apparently, had dressed himself in their skins.

A break in the text makes it impossible to give the opening lines of Uta-Napishtim's reply, but he mentions the father and mother of Gilgamish, and in the last twenty lines of the Tenth Tablet he warns Gilgamish that on earth there is nothing permanent, that Mammitum, the arranger of destinies, has settled the question of the death and life of man with the Anunnaki, and that none may find out the day of his death or escape from death.

## The Eleventh Tablet.

The story of the Deluge as told by Uta-Napishtim to Gilgamish has already been given on pp. 31-40, and we therefore pass on to the remaining contents of this Tablet. When Uta-Napishtim had finished the story of the Deluge, he said to Gilgamish, " Now as touching thyself ; which of the gods " will gather thee to himself so that thou mayest find the life " which thou seekest ? Come now, do not lay thyself down " to sleep for six days and seven nights." But in spite of this admonition as soon as Gilgamish had sat down, drowsiness overpowered him and he fell fast asleep. Uta-Napishtim, seeing that even the mighty hero Gilgamish could not resist falling asleep, with some amusement drew the attention of his wife to the fact, but she felt sorry for the tired man, and suggested that he should take steps to help him to return to his home. In reply Uta-Napishtim told her to bake bread for him and she did so, and each day for six days she carried a loaf to the ship and laid it on the deck where Gilgamish lay sleeping. On the seventh day when she took the loaf Uta-Napishtim touched Gilgamish, and the hero woke up with a start, and admitted that he had been overcome with sleep, and made incapable of movement thereby.

Still vexed with the thought of death and filled with anxiety to escape from it, Gilgamish asked his host what he should do and where he should go to effect his object. By Uta-Napishtim's advice, he made an agreement with Ur-Shanabi the boatman, and prepared to re-cross the sea on his way home. But before he set out on his way Uta-Napishtim told him of the existence of a plant which grew at the bottom of the sea, and apparently led Gilgamish to believe that the possession of it would confer upon him immortality. Thereupon Gilgamish tied heavy stones [to his feet], and let himself down into the sea through an opening in the floor of the boat. When he reached the bottom of the sea, he saw the plant and plucked it, and ascended into the boat with it. Showing it to Ur-Shanabi, he told him that it was a most marvellous plant, and that it would enable a man to obtain his heart's desire. Its name was "Shîbu iṣṣaḫir amelu," ⟨⊦ ⊭ ⩔⊢ ⊣⟩ ⟩⟩ ⊭⟨⊣ ⊭⫶, *i.e.*, "The old man becometh young [again]," and Gilgamish declared that he would "eat of it in order to recover his lost youth," and that he would take it home to his fortified city of Erech. Misfortune, however, dogged his steps, and the plant never reached Erech, for whilst Gilgamish and Ur-Shanabi were on their way back to Erech they passed a pool the water of which was very cold, and Gilgamish dived into it and took a bath. Whilst there a serpent discovered the whereabouts of the plant through its smell and swallowed it. When Gilgamish saw what had happened he cursed aloud, and sat down and wept, and the tears coursed down his cheeks as he lamented over the waste of his toil, and the vain expenditure of his heart's blood, and his failure to do any good for himself. Disheartened and weary he struggled on his way with his friend, and at length they arrived at the fortified city of Erech.[1]

---

[1] The city of Erech was the second of the four cities which, according to Genesis x, 10, were founded by Nimrod, the son of Cush, the "mighty hunter before the Lord. And the beginning of his kingdom was Babel, and Erech and Accad, and Calneh, in the land of Shinar." The Sumerians and Babylonians called the city "URUK KI" ⩔⫶⟩ ⟨⊨⟩; the first sign means "dwelling" or "habitation," and the second "land, country," etc., and we may regard it as the "inhabited country," *par excellence*, of Lower Babylonia at a very early period. The site of Erech is well-known, and is marked by the vast ruins which the Arabs call "Warkah," or Al-Warkah. These lie in 31° 19′ N. Lat. and 45° 40′ E. Long., and are about four miles from the Euphrates, on the left or east bank of the river. Sir W. K. Loftus carried out excavations on the site in 1849–52, and says that the external walls

## 56  THE EPIC OF GILGAMISH.

Then Gilgamish told Ur-Shanabi to jump up on the wall and examine the bricks from the foundations to the battlements, and see if the plans which he had made concerning them had been carried out during his absence.

### The Twelfth Tablet.

The text of the Twelfth Tablet is very fragmentary, and contains large gaps, but it seems certain that Gilgamish did not abandon his hope of finding the secret of immortality. He had failed to find it upon earth, and he made arrangements with the view of trying to find it in the kingdom of the dead. The priests whom he consulted described to him the conditions under which he might hope to enter the Underworld, but he was unable to fulfil the obligations which they laid upon him, and he could not go there. Gilgamish then thought that if he could have a conversation with Enkidu, his dead friend, he might learn from him what he wanted to know. He appealed to Bêl and asked him to raise up the spirit of Enkidu for him, but Bêl made no answer; he then appealed to Sin, and this

---

of sun-dried brick enclosing the main portion of the ruins form an irregular circle five and a half miles in circumference; in places they are from 40 to 50 feet in height, and they seem to have been about 20 feet thick. The turrets on the wall were semi-oval in shape, and about 50 feet apart. The principal ruin is that of the Ziggurat, or temple tower, which in 1850 was 100 feet high and 200 feet square. Loftus calls it "Buwáríya," *i.e.*, " reed mats," because reed mats were used in its construction, but *búrîyah*, " rush mat," is a Persian not Arabic word, and the name is more probably connected with the Arabic " Bawâr," *i.e.*, " ruin," " place of death," etc. This tower stood in a courtyard which was 350 feet long and 270 feet wide. The next large ruin is that which is called " Waṣwaṣ " (plur. Waṣâwiṣ"), *i.e.*, " large stone." The "Waṣwaṣ" referred to was probably the block of columnar basalt which Loftus and Mr. T. K. Lynch found projecting through the soil; on it was sculptured the figure of a warrior, and the stone itself was regarded as a talisman by the natives. This ruin is 246 feet long, 174 feet wide and 80 feet high. On three sides of it are terraces of different elevations, but the south-west side presents a perpendicular façade, at one place 23 feet in height. For further details see Loftus, *Chaldea and Susiana*, London, 1857, p. 159 ff. Portions of the ruins of Warkah were excavated by the German archaeologists in 1914, and large " finds " of tablets and other antiquities are said to have been made.

god also made no answer. He next appealed to Ea, who, taking pity on him, ordered the warrior god Nergal to produce the spirit of Enkidu, and this god opened a hole in the ground through which the spirit of Enkidu passed up into this world "like a breath of wind." Gilgamish began to ask the spirit of Enkidu questions, but gained very little information or satisfaction. The last lines of the tablet seem to say that the spirit of the unburied man reposeth not in the earth, and that the spirit of the friendless man wandereth about the streets eating the remains of food which are cast out from the cooking pots.

E. A. WALLIS BUDGE.

DEPARTMENT OF EGYPTIAN AND ASSYRIAN
ANTIQUITIES, BRITISH MUSEUM,
*July* 24*th*, 1920.

## NOTE.

The Trustees of the British Museum have published large selections of cuneiform texts from the cylinders, tablets, etc., that were found in the ruins of Nineveh by Layard, Rassam, Smith and others, in the following works:—

CUNEIFORM INSCRIPTIONS OF WESTERN ASIA. Vol. I. 1861. Fol. 1*l*. (Out of print.)
——— Vol. II. 1866. Fol. 1*l*. (Out of print.)
——— Vol. III. 1870. Fol. 1*l*.
——— Vol. IV. Second edition. 1891. Fol. 1*l*. (Out of print.)
——— Vol. V. Plates I.–XXXV. 1880. Fol. 10*s*. 6*d*. (Out of print.)
——— Vol. V. Plates XXXVI–LXX. 1884. Fol. 10*s*. 6*d*. (Out of print.)
——— Vol. V. Plates I.–LXX. Lithographed reprint. 1909. Fol. 1*l*. 7*s*.

INSCRIPTIONS FROM ASSYRIAN MONUMENTS. 1851. Fol. 1*l*. 1*s*.

CUNEIFORM TEXTS FROM BABYLONIAN TABLETS, &C., IN THE BRITISH MUSEUM. Parts I.–V., VII.–XXIII., XXV., XXVII.–XXXIV. 50 plates each. 1896–1914. 7*s*. 6*d*. each.
——— Part VI. 49 plates. 1898. 7*s*. 6*d*.
——— Part XXIV. 50 plates. 1908. Fol. 10*s*.
——— Part XXVI. 54 plates. 1909. Fol. 12*s*.

ANNALS OF THE KINGS OF ASSYRIA. Cuneiform texts with transliterations and translations. Vol. I. 1903. 4to. 1*l*.

CATALOGUE OF THE CUNEIFORM TABLETS IN THE KOUYUNJIK COLLECTION. Vol. I. 8vo. 1889. 15*s*.
——— Vol. II. 1891. 15*s*.
——— Vol. III. 1894. 15*s*.
——— Vol. IV. 1896. 1*l*.
——— Vol. V. 1899. 1*l*. 3*s*.
——— Supplement. 8vo. 1914. 1*l*.

Harrison & Sons, Ltd.,
*Printers in Ordinary to His Majesty,*
St. Martin's Lane, London, W.C. 2.

www.ingramcontent.com/pod-product-compliance
Lightning Source LLC
Chambersburg PA
CBHW081328040426
42453CB00013B/2341